Between Sanctity and Sand

poems by

Yael S. Hacohen

Finishing Line Press
Georgetown, Kentucky

Between Sanctity
and Sand

Copyright © 2021 by Yael S. Hacohen
ISBN 978-1-64662-470-6 First Edition
All rights reserved under International and Pan-American Copyright Conventions. No part of this book may be reproduced in any manner whatsoever without written permission from the publisher, except in the case of brief quotations embodied in critical articles and reviews.

ACKNOWLEDGMENTS

I want to thank the journal editors and poetry competitions that first featured my poems, sometimes in a different form and under different titles:

The Poetry Review: "The Weight of a Jericho 941" and "What I Forgot from My Wars"
Prairie Schooner: "Peace"
Bellevue Literary Review, "I Never Saw a Wild Thing Sorry for Itself"
MSLexia Poetry Prize for Women, "Michal Doesn't Like Ants"
Consequence Prize in Poetry, "Identity Card"
The Wrath-Bearing Tree, "Between Sanctity and Sand"
Nine Lines Review, "The First Time Rockets Fall in Tel Aviv"
Treehouse, "My Boots"

Publisher: Leah Huete de Maines
Editor: Christen Kincaid
Cover Art: Daniel Goldfarb
Author Photo: Liron Erel
Cover Design: Elizabeth Maines McCleavy

Order online: www.finishinglinepress.com
also available on amazon.com

Author inquiries and mail orders:
Finishing Line Press
PO Box 1626
Georgetown, Kentucky 40324
USA

Table of Contents

The Weight of a Jericho 941 1

What I Forgot from My Wars 2

Peace 3

Goliath 4

Settlement 5

I Never Saw a Wild Thing Sorry for Itself 7

Michal Doesn't Like Ants 8

Grit 9

I Once Stood 10

Identity Card 12

Alive 13

Between Sanctity and Sand 14

Good Training 15

Not the Wave but the Force of the Water 16

The First Time Rockets Fall in Tel Aviv 17

Timshol 18

My Boots 19

*For Yuval and Tamar, who wake up every morning laughing,
and for Uri, who taught them joy.*

The Weight of a Jericho 941

It happens when your nine-millimeter round
gets lodged in the chamber. It could be the dust, maybe,
or you just didn't put in the time to clean it.
No. It happens when you're sitting on the wooden chair,
at the crowded café, waiting for the waitress to bring over a salad.
And you notice that the tattooed birds on her wrist are flying away, but
you don't know where they're going.
I say, you notice the wrist but don't notice the man running in.
After he shoots, you want to shoot back, but you didn't
put in the time. And now you can't get your breathing straight.
You know your handgun like you know Tuesdays, like rain.
But you can't get that first bullet dislodged.
And you can't help but think of her sparrows finally flocking,
either north or south along the flyway.

What I Forgot from My Wars

Let the night come & lay your head under
a blanket of dust. An orb of mosquitoes radios
your position. Let them sing.

Even in the desert, the white capparis flowers
hold their stomachs as if they had been shot.
The larks of your mind are still cleaning, scrubbing.

Shooting is the cleaning of black oil into & out of.
You want to place your uniform on the shelf, one
sleeve at a time. Brush your hair into years.

You trace the outlines of your breath, as you
would a child's back. Say—it's safe now;
Say—I've got you. Hush your marching

& witness the constellation of canvas tents fill
with tens of girls in their cots, whispering to themselves
(or each other) the lullabies their mothers spoke.

Peace

Listen, even the olive tree
needs to be beaten with a stick.

Goliath

The real tragedy of that cloudy day took
place when the eleven-foot man
watched a red-head boy running at him
with a wooden stick, an oversized coat of
mail, a helmet bobbing around loosely on
his head.
And in a deep voice like a field,
as only a father would, he said to the boy
go home son, just go home.
Goliath, he refused to believe
even when he finally saw the rock.

Settlement

I know a line of olive trees
        In a field when I lift the shield

Over my brow. The shield
        Is like a peacock, heavy

And unlike a peacock, I watch
        As the husband holds onto

The frame of the door
        With his fingertips.

I am told this is for peace
        & when the son crashes

Into my shield, I do not
        Back down. I advance

Sideways, or with a different
        Shade of paint. I push my right

Leg forward & the line of my
        Men & women

Quickly closes ranks.
        Not even a blue feather could

Fit between us. These
        Men & women are my family.

I would die, but not die.
        I am told this land has always belonged

To Palestine. These are their fields,
        Their olive trees. No Israeli

Can live here. I recall the wife
        Attempts to approach our line

She says, we speak the same
        Flag, me and her. She ties

A ribbon to my shield and
        I do not remove it.

I am ordered to evacuate this
        Family by force. No Israeli can

Live here, they tell me. I raise
        The shield as if to protect her

Before ramming it into
        The side of her face. My line

Of men & women has my back
        Always, and they tell me so.

The husband sees this
        & releases the wooden frame.

He bends into a question
        On the ground.

I Never Saw a Wild Thing Sorry for Itself

When your CO singles you out in Krav Maga,
you'd better throw a punch, little girl.
Make your fist sing its soft *goddamn*
smashing into the bridge of his nose.
He'll bob and weave, take out his clip
and whack it right into your skull. Don't cry.
Not even in the barracks. Not even now.

Michal Doesn't Like Ants

Michal doesn't like ants, the smell of sweat, nor the color yellow, or sand, pears, bananas, green vegetables, orange vegetables, windows you can't see into, grinding teeth, the sound of swallowing, triangles, octagons, heart shapes, buses, taxies.

Michal bicycles the same route on Mondays, Tuesdays, and Thursdays. On Wednesdays, she preferred the seafront. Michal doesn't notice people much—for example, on that Wednesday she didn't notice the man entering "Porcupine Café" on the Tel-Aviv promenade with nervous eyes.

When the blast wave hit, Michal wasn't hunched. The explosion circled the air for a fifth of a second. She felt the convulsion of her eardrum, of her heart muscle, of her stomach. The blaze lit the café; within forty seconds, the air was welling in thickness. Paper scraps, shards of glass, a hat, drops of blood, white broken mugs, drifted sand, and driblets of water could be found on the floor.

Michal remembered only that she had read that Fight or Flight takes only three seconds to initiate. The time it takes to pucker your lips, to focus a camera, fourteen rat heartbeats. The time it takes an African Horn Lizard to eat forty-five ants one at a time.

Grit

You work to plant a new thing, but this is not the work of planting. You bend down in the middle of a barren plot to remove a large granite stone from the ground. The stone is not heavy, & you are surprised. You place the stone in the back of the truck, on top of the pile of stones. You walk not half-a-pace before you bend down again. You work in silence, or perhaps you curse. The hours pass, & the small pile grows taller. No stone looks the same, but they don't seem that different. You resent the pile, resent the plot. The day stretches before you, & sweat drips down the slope of your back, your thighs. It pools above your lip & mixes with the dirt. This is the work of all grief, & you understand there is no excitement in it.

I Once Stood

In the great hall
Of Bahad 1,
When I finished
Commander's Course.
It was a Friday
And the dust disappeared
The air was not
Yellow anymore
But light blue,
Like how the wind
Can stop screaming
For a moment,
And the world is still.
Except, on
That Friday—
The wind wasn't still,
It was screeching
And pulling,
The branches
From their scalps.
But the air,
The air was
Light blue
Or maybe clear.
In any case,
The day was warm.
It was warm
As if it remembered
All the things I
Had to do to finish
And was blushing
At the cheeks.
As if it could recall,
The waiting
Hour after hour
On the night watch,

And how I
Finished first
In Navigation week,
How I tripped
And knocked loose
My front tooth,
And that misfire
My CO
Kept screaming,
But the shot
Went so
Close to my ear,
I swear I couldn't
Make out
A single word
He said.
It was always
Dusty in that place,
But not
That day.
That day,
I stood
Amongst my peers
And my CO
Pinned the pin
On my lapel
And I swear,
I think,
It must have been
I swear,
It had to be
The clearest day
I've ever seen.

Identity Card

I was a farmer from *Nahallal*.
I walked barefoot across the fields

if I could—
between flights of stairs if I could not.

Everywhere I went I was always a grateful Russian
who favored good fortune and good health.

And I was a Pole, when I sit in the shade of an olive
tree, I spread the napkin evenly on my thighs.

Always looking over my shoulder;
even the snow could not erase 1942.

I was a proud Austrian,
I would not hesitate to throw a punch.

I was always a white crane from Egypt
spreading my wings in search of land.

I will not deny in every case I was a Palestinian—
my brothers who believe in the sword and believe in the flag;

I was a Jew; I look within the corners of the letters
for the comfort of the sky.

Above all, I was an Israeli from *Tzhala*.
I heard the footsteps of my father, of his father,

of their fathers—and I will listen,
till it is my turn to speak.

Alive

       I once knew a boy who crushed the legs of a dung beetle,
            in the afternoon. The beetle was solemn as a
                    cartridge.
Its dark body ascended on the beach like a Jewish refugee
            in the *Hapalla*, slow and determined.
The boy picked up a wooden stick and crushed its tiny legs.
        As if the boy wasn't a
        soldier who watched his friend
        get shot in the stomach.
How the friend remained standing, like a building with a rain gutter,
            the insides spilling out onto the street.
      The boy crushed the insect's legs, one at a time.
          It was merciful. It was joyous.
The dung beetle was never even alive
                    until right then.

Between Sanctity and Sand

The first time I shot an M-16
it was the heat of summer in the Negev.
Gas-operated with a rotating bolt, five-point-fifty
six caliber, with nineteen bullets a box.
And I could shoot like an angel.
I could hit a running target
at six-hundred-fifty meters.
I hummed to myself as I shot,
I was eighteen.
The retama flower of my hair-bun drawn back tight
blooming, sprouting open with every green round.

Good Training

I pull the pin out of the grenade.
I can feel its dead weight.
I'm holding the thing when it explodes.
There's a ringing, a brass taste
like salt water taffy.
Slow as rock debris, my CO's helmet hammers
into my shoulder, knocking me down.
He's on top of me, crushing my ribs.
mouthing words I can't make out.

As if I'm wearing pink pajamas, I hear the deep voice
of my father reading from Amichai:
When my head hit the door, I cried
"my head, my head", and cried "door, door"
and did not cry "mother", and not "god."
I did not wish the end of days
to be a world with no more heads and doors.

Not the Wave but the Force of the Water

Itai was from the city of Haifa, where streets are wide as summer. Red bougainvillea and hibiscus intertwine on hedges between the buildings. He lived two stoplights from the ocean, and the smell of the waves, the salt, and the hermit crabs soaked every corner of the city. Itai had already lived to see his ninetieth birthday, but his face retained its muscular shape, like a well-made ship. He was born into fear, and from fear he made his living. He worked as a lawyer, filing motions, reading briefs, ironing his shirts, & the city was the same. Perhaps the city and Itai were so similar that one might be mistaken for the other. Since Itai was alive and awake for most of his hours, he might take the place of the city when the city lay down its head to sleep, and in exchange the city would replace Itai when he was making love. So similar they were that it was rumored that Haifa was from the man Itai, and finally no one could tell which was living and which was a fiction from the start.

The First Time Rockets Fall in Tel Aviv

Uri isn't home. I run outside to see. *Clink*, the soft betrayal of the door locking behind me, sirens mutter prayers. I'm on my knees. "Please, door, let me in, please."

Timshol

You haven't scored your first goal.
Aced a test. Sneaked a peek at the girl's locker room.
Haven't tasted the warmth of Fairuz's voice in
person.
Haven't seen a woman, with her brown hair resting on your chest.
You couldn't know how it feels to move in with her,
to pick the colors of the curtains, the chairs, the bed.
Little boy, what could lead you to strap a bomb to your chest?
The only word I know in Arabic, *Sharha*.
Explain. I would have listened for as long as it takes.

My Boots

Each year in Ramat Hagolan, at least 1,200 cattle produce milk, feed on grain and oats, give birth, and die when their time comes. When the cows were under Syrian control, they were spoken to in Arabic, and after Israel took control of the land in 1973, in the war of Yom Kippur, the cows of that region were spoken to in Hebrew, or Arabic. Depending on the farmer.

In the year 1997, a calf was born. She was the second-born heifer of a prize-winning cow and died by stepping on a mine. This could be where the story ended, if not for a change in the family business. It was exactly the month that the family that owned the calf decided its skin would be used for leather.

They called in a specialist, who was missing half a pinky from his days as an apprentice. The specialist stood in the middle of the green field and produced a sheathed knife. The knife was curved like a quarter moon. He worked with the utmost care so as not to leave a scratch. The skin came off in a single thin sheet, like the parting of red petals.

The leather was loaded onto a truck. It was removed and spread in a large metal container by the two agile hands of the craftsman. He noted that the skin was small in size and heavy in weight: perfect for a small woman's combat boots.

The leather was laid out on a black rubber cutting mat, and a pattern was drawn. Using a trimming knife, the craftsman traced the leather as one would trace a lover's back, until four symmetrical pieces lay detached.

The pieces were handed over to a young shoemaker who worked the leather into shape and attached it to a rubber sole. The letter "צ" was stamped at the top, where it was closest to God. A small pocket for dog-tags was added into the strip. Finally, they were shipped to a base in HaKiryaa.

It happened that, in the year 2006, a bushy-browed Nagad chose them off the shelf, tied the shoelaces together in a timely manner, and threw them in the back of his truck. Fate called me in to see the Nagad, who whispered like a boy with a crush: "I have a surprise for you".

Friends died in that time, but they wore different shoes. My boots were never shot, were never punctured, were never crushed. They only lifted one foot after the other, or both at once.

Additional Acknowledgments

I would like to devote special thanks to the MFA Creative Writing program at New York University, the best two years of my creative life. In my first semester, I took a course from the poet Professor Craig Morgan Teicher, who through thought-provoking discussions and indispensable intellectual guidance empowered me to use my voice. Professor Teicher's professional genius, kind personality, and commitment make him a truly exceptional mentor. It was Charlie Simic, my Professor at NYU, who told me that the only way to be a poet was to write poems. So many of these poems were written under his sharp and humorous guidance. These poems would not have been possible without the mentorship of the brilliant Professor Yusef Komunyakaa, who told me, "the ear never lies", and whose poetry is a burning light for me to live by. I am grateful to have been a part of the workshop with the incomparable, generous Professor Catherine Barnett, who taught me to read, as if for the first time. My time at NYU would not have been what it was without the incredible Professor Edward Hirsch, whose knowledge of poetry is awe-inspiring and whose kindness permeated our collaboration. Heading this program at the time, with her radiant presence, was none other than Professor Deborah Landau, whose generosity and continued support I owe so much to.

It's an honor to thank the weekly New York University Veterans Writing Workshop for their fellowship and support. During my time there, I met with veterans who have shaped my poetry and whom I consider my brothers and sisters. I want to especially thank Zachary, Jennifer, Maurice, Omri, Drew, Nichole, Brian, Jesse, Jonathan, Adam, Tom, Nebojsa, Anthony, Derek, and Teresa, without whom I would have never had the courage or fire to write these poems.

I would like to thank my Chair at UC Berkeley, Professor Marianne Constable, who always made room for my poetry in her intellectual and kind conversations with me. Her support for me, in all my avenues and endeavors, has meant everything to me. I also want to thank Professor Michael Mascuch, Professor Catherine Albiston, and my poetry angel Professor Susan Schweik, who have all encouraged me to pursue rhetoric in all its forms.

On a personal note, I want to thank my sisters Gil, Oren, and Adi, who are the most powerful women I've ever met. My two grandmothers: Zivia and Ilana: you are my inspiration. And finally, my parents Ronny and Dan, you are the guiding lights by which I stride. I could not be prouder to be your daughter.

Yael Hacohen is a PhD student at the Department of Rhetoric at UC Berkeley, where she studies contemporary women's and nonbinary people's war poetry in the United States and Israel. She is especially interested in poetics that challenge the traditional male-centered corpus of war poetry. At UC Berkeley, Hacohen has taught undergraduate courses on illegitimate violence and memory, identity, and lyricality in cybernetic culture.

Hacohen received her MFA in Poetry from New York University, where she wrote her creative thesis under the guidance of the poet Craig Morgan Teicher. At NYU, Hacohen taught an undergrad course focused on translations of internationally acclaimed works. Additionally, Hacohen served as the International Editor at the *Washington Square Review*, a nationally distributed literary journal. During her time at NYU, Hacohen was awarded the NYU Veterans Workshop Fellowship, leading a weekly writing workshop for recent veterans of the wars in Iraq and Afghanistan. There she also served as the Editor-in-Chief for *Nine Lines Literary Review*, which was created by the participants of the workshop and devoted to literature by veterans of the wars in Iraq and Afghanistan.

Her poetry, short stories, and translations appear in many publications, journals, and competitions, including *Prairie Schooner, The Poetry Review, Bellevue Literary Review*, and *Every Day Poets Magazine*. She was a finalist in the 2015 Glimmer Train Very Short Story Competition and for the 2015 Consequence Prize in Poetry and the 2013 MSLexia Poetry Prize for Women.

As a lieutenant in the Israeli Army, Hacohen served as an intelligence officer in the 36 Northern War Room and later as an intelligence officer in the 162nd Armor Division.

www.ingramcontent.com/pod-product-compliance
Lightning Source LLC
LaVergne TN
LVHW041521070426
835507LV00012B/1735